How You Do
Anything
Is How You Do
Everything

-A Workbook-

Dedicated to "Toughie"
beloved friend and teacher

Books by Cheri Huber and Ashwini Narayanan

Don't Suffer, Communicate! A Zen Guide to Compassionate Communication
The Big Bamboozle: How You Get Conned Out of the Life You Want and What to Do about It
What Universe Are You Creating? Zen and the Art of Recording and Listening
I Don't Want To, I Don't Feel Like It: How Resistance Controls Your Life and What to Do about It
Published by Keep It Simple Books

Books by Cheri Huber

There Is Nothing Wrong with You: Going Beyond Self-Hate, Rev. Ed.
What You Practice Is What You Have: A Guide to Having the Life You Want
The Fear Book: Facing Fear Once and for All
The Depression Book: Depression as an Opportunity for Spiritual Growth
Be the Person You Want to Find: Relationship and Self-Discovery
How You Do Anything Is How You Do Everything: A Workbook
The Key and the Name of the Key Is Willingness
Suffering Is Optional: Three Keys to Freedom and Joy
When You're Falling, Dive: Acceptance, Possibility and Freedom
There Is Nothing Wrong With You for Teens
Nothing Happens Next: Responses to Questions about Meditation
Time-Out for Parents: A Guide to Compassionate Parenting, Rev. Ed.
Transform Your Life: A Year of Awareness Practice
Trying to Be Human: Zen Talks, edited by Sara Jenkins
Sweet Zen: Dharma Talks with Cheri Huber, edited by Sara Jenkins
Good Life: Zen Precepts Retreat with Cheri Huber, edited by Sara Jenkins
The Zen Monastery Cookbook: Stories and Recipes from a Zen Kitchen
There Are No Secrets: Zen Meditation with Cheri Huber (DVD)
Published by Keep It Simple Books

Forthcoming Ebooks

Don't Suffer, Communicate!
Sweet Zen
Trying to Be Human
There Is Nothing Wrong with You

How to Get from Where You Are to Where You Want to Be
Published by Hay House

Unconditional Self-Acceptance: A Do-It-Yourself Course (6 CD set)
Published by Sounds True

Introduction

It is not possible to do this workbook wrong. This book is simply an opportunity for you to see a little more clearly how you are as a person, how you approach life, and how you choose your values and beliefs, and this is not a realm in which right and wrong apply.

This workbook focuses on the "process" of you, not the particulars, the content of your life. What you do or believe or feel will not be the point; how you do it will be the point. If you observed how you do this workbook, you would probably learn more about who and how you are than you could learn from the content of the exercises. How you do anything is how you do everything.

An example: you might hold the belief that "life is sacred," a simple statement. This book will encourage you to explore how you know that. Who taught you to believe that? How does believing that affect your life? Does it help you in not suffering, or does it cause you to suffer? What happens if someone challenges that belief? Why do we have beliefs? What if they're not true? And so on...not to encourage you to do or not do anything about your beliefs, but to encourage you to explore the whole process of believing and how believing affects you.

Life involves suffering. Here, we define suffering as everything from displeasure or dissatisfaction to tragic loss or utter failure. The four causes of suffering:

1. not getting what you want
2. getting what you want and not being satisfied with it
3. having to endure the absence of those or that which you love
4. having to endure the presence of those or that which you do not love

How we are and how we conduct our lives leads either toward suffering or away from suffering. Throughout this book you will be encouraged to see how you do what you do and asked to question whether your process causes you suffering or leads away from it. This is the purpose of this workbook.

We are not suggesting that you make any decisions, just become aware. Notice everything. See if you can allow yourself to be exactly as you are with as few judgements as possible for the duration of this project. Of course, there will be judgment! See if you can become more interested in the process of judging than in what is being judged.

This book is for you. Your answers aren't going to be graded. How you are is who you are. Comparing yourself to anyone is like comparing broccoli and baseball bats. No comparison is possible. And, of course there will be comparisons. Just see if you can become more interested in the process of comparing than in what is being compared.

Knowing how you are is the beginning of freedom, and it is true that looking inward, seeing ourselves, can be scary. If the opportunity arises, see if you can give yourself permission to be scared, resistant, angry, upset, frustrated, sad, and depressed, as well as happy, excited, eager, open, and willing.

And please, if you decide to approach this workbook, do so with all of the compassion for yourself that you can find. You are probably not a great artist or writer or psychologist or spiritual adept. So don't expect to draw like Leonardo da Vinci, write like Jane Austen, analyze like Carl Jung, or have insights like the Buddha.

Just enjoy getting to know you a little better.

Draw a picture of life.

4.

What were the most important steps
that brought you to where you are today?

In many of these exercises your answers depend on "who" does the exercise. Some people describe this as playing different roles, wearing different hats, or following different scripts. We are different ways at different times with different people. For instance, if your boss said "there's something I need to talk to you about," you probably wouldn't respond that same way as if your best friend said that same thing. A different person dresses up and takes a date to the movies than the one who watches reruns on the couch in their pajamas.

We use the word "subpersonality" to denote the various aspects of the personality, such as Athlete, Perfectionist, Lover, Daydreamer, Mother's Helper, Gossip, Critic, etc. We go in and out of these aspects constantly and we have many common expressions that indicate the changes: "I am not myself today," "Part of me wants to go but part of me doesn't," "I'm going to put myself on a diet." Even an emotional response like anger or sadness will be different with each aspect.

We find it helpful to give names to subpersonalities, gentle, loving names, even to the parts of the personality that seem not to serve us well. These exercises often ask you to "name the part of yourself who..." to help get a sense of the movement between various facets of yourself.

6.

Draw a picture of yourself at work.

⇩ Describe the qualities of this person. ⇩

DRAW A PICTURE OF YOURSELF AT PLAY.
 - Describe the qualities of this person-

8.

 Draw a picture of yourself at home.

Describe the qualities of this person.

Where do you want to be in 5 years?

10 years?

15 years?

20 years?

What are you doing now that will lead to that?

What are you doing that will keep you from that?

Looking at yourself...

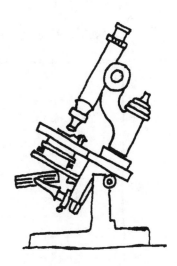

What I've been told about me...

What I tell myself about me...

What I really know about me...

12.

What would make your life perfect?

What do you choose instead?

Write a horoscope for yourself for the coming year.

14.

What happens to you when you feel uncomfortable?

How do you avoid discomfort?

What do you have in your life and what do you exclude from your
life in order to avoid discomfort?

See if you can avoid the tendency to use your answers as an opportunity to entertain criticism. Criticism keeps us stuck. Criticism does not cause us to improve.

Beatings do not cause us to improve.

Simply add awareness of how you want your life to be and begin to notice how you stop yourself from having that.

Often it seems that just being aware isn't enough. We're very conditioned to believe that to have what we want in life requires that we do something. That desire to "do" keeps us stuck. When we see how we keep ourselves from having what we want and from being who we choose to be, we find that we already have everything we need and that we are inherently the person we choose to be.

Just watch.

When you see clearly what you're doing and how you're doing it,
you'll also know why,
and that it's not working,
and you'll simply stop.

Think of something you want.

⇧ Write it down or draw it in here. ⇧

☆ What are you doing to get/have that? ☆

☆ What are you doing to get in your way? ☆

How are you when you get what you want?

How are you when you don't get what you want?

HOW DO YOU KEEP FROM HAVING WHAT YOU WANT?

— Spend some time on this one. —

What did you get
that you're not satisfied with
that's causing you to want
what you're wanting now?

The Four Causes of Suffering

- Not getting what you want

- getting what you want and not being satisfied with it

- Having to endure the absence of those or that which you love

- Having to endure the presence of those or that which you do not love

SEE THE KEY, PAGES 20-23

When we find ourselves in circumstances we don't like, our assumption is that we need to change something, fix things. Changing externals never resolves a problem. We all know the experience of disliking a job, a type of person, a certain atmosphere, etc., and leaving only to find ourselves in the same situation somewhere else.

When we look closely we usually see that the source of the difficulty comes down to wanting things not to be the way they are. We are afraid that if we accept things as they are, that very act will mean they won't change, they'll be that way forever, and we'll be unhappy. There are actually several untrue assumptions operating:

1) I don't like it, therefore something is wrong with it.

2) As long as it's this way, I can't be happy (safe, content, etc.).

3) Resisting the way it is will cause it to change.

4) Accepting means it will always be that way and I'll be unhappy.

We fail to see that resisting what is is the problem. Our well-being is not dependent on any external. We think it is, but it is not. For instance: "I hate my job because my boss is a jerk." It's easy to think that is a true statement and to believe:

1) I have to quit my job, or

2) I have to hang on, hating her/him and hoping s/he leaves, or

3) I have to stay and be willing to suffer until I can retire.

Not so. I also have the option of accepting the whole situation (boss included) exactly as it is.

The wonderful part is that at the moment we accept what is, it changes. The circumstances might or might not be the same; our experience of them will be different.

List the ten things that are most important to you.

one	two
three	four
five	six
seven	eight
nine	ten

Let yourself recall a holiday.

Draw the experience, realistically and/or symbolically.

See yourself approaching the holidays...

What are you saying?	What are you doing?

What are you feeling?	What are you hoping for?

What are you afraid of?

You are having a very special person spend
the holidays with you.

How would you like it to be?

How are you if it doesn't happen that way?

How could you make it be the way you really want it to be?

26.

Write a dialogue between the part of you who likes holidays and the part who dislikes holidays. Can you name the parts?

What do you need to work on?

⇧ WRITE IT DOWN IN HERE. ⇧
⇩ FIVE QUESTIONS ⇩

1. How is this currently apparent in your life?

2. How has this been an ongoing process in your life?

3. What would you need to do to resolve it?

4. What are you willing to do to resolve it?

5. What are the pay-offs, positive and negative, for not resolving it?

+ POSITIVE +	− NEGATIVE −

(A gift)→ You can have anything in the world...

· What is it?

· How did you select it?

· What did you consider and not select?

· How will you feel having it?

· How will you be different?

· List the qualities of the gift you have selected. 🎀

Are these missing in your life currently?

Think of your most favorite and least favorite animal.

Write a story about them that uses the adjectives that show why you like and dislike each. (The gentle, kindhearted dog lifted her intelligent head and surveyed the sneaky, stupid...)

STRIPED
SKUNK

BLACK
BEAR

QUAIL

MOUNTAIN
LION

Can you own these qualities?

If money were no object...

Where would you go?

With whom would you go?

What would you do?

Think of the secrets you keep...

Who do you consider telling?

Who do you specifically not tell?

What/Who are you protecting?

⇨ What would people think if they knew? ⇦

can you see how you feel these things about yourself, and can you be open to the possibility that others might not feel that way and don't have your values at all?

Think of a character from history, fiction or fantasy.
Write a story about this character in action.

Own the story as your story
and the character as a part of yourself.

Write a dialogue between you and the character.

Are you a compassionate person?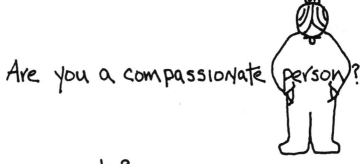

When are you most compassionate?

When are you least compassionate?

Are you more compassionate with yourself or others?

What is the most loving, compassionate thing you could do for yourself right now?

What do you believe about yourself and life that keeps you from doing this?

WHO YOU ARE RIGHT NOW...

How do you feel? How old?	What do you think about life?
How would you change your life?	How would you change others?
What do you want?	What do you need?

Do this exercise regularly to get a sense of your changing selves.

38.

What are your strengths

and weaknesses?

How do you know that's what they are? Who says so?

What do you <u>need</u> in order to be happy?

— Get picky with this one. Give details. Elaborate. Carry on at length. Draw pictures. Name names. —

What do you <u>really</u> need in order to be happy?

List the greatest moments in your life.

Do this exercise with all the courage you can muster.
Be as fearless as possible.

I now give myself permission to...

Think of three dominant characteristics of someone you dislike.
Write them down.

1.

2.

3.

Think of three dominant characteristics of someone you like.
Write them down.

1.

2.

3.

Can you own those and see how you are like that, too?

These are postures, attitudes, and beliefs that you have learned and now cling to. Look to see how many of them bring happiness to your relationships and how many lead to unhappiness. Would you let go of them in order to have happy relationships?

What do other people expect from you?

They expect me to...

The standards by which we think others are judging us are the standards by which we are judging others.

46.

This is what we call the "double reverse projection." I project onto you what I think about myself, and then I think you think that about me. I project my standards onto you and then believe you are judging me by my standards.

P.S. If the standards by which you are judging me are not the same as mine, it will never occur to me that you are judging me about those things!

At the end of the day,

review your day,

recall each interaction throughout the day,

"...and then she said"

describe each person you encountered.

Remember what they were doing, how they were acting.

SEE THE KEY, PAGES 77-84

Can you own those projections? Can you see how you are that way?

Imagine that you're going away.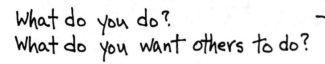

What do you do?
What do you want others to do?

Imagine that someone else is going away.

What do you do?
What do you want them to do?

What book, song, and movie best describe your life?

📖

🎼

🎥

What would you title a book, a song, and a movie about your life?

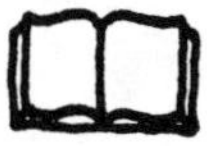

📖

🎼

🎥

Tense yourself physically.

Relax.

Tense emotionally.

Relax.

Tense mentally.

Relax.

Repeat each exercise as you find out
exactly where and how you do this.

Draw a picture of your body.

Move your attention
from the top of your head,

down through your entire body,

all the way to your toes,

and experience your body as fully as possible.

What kind of body is it?

How do you feel about it?

Is it comfortable to you?

How would you change it?

What do you value most?

What do you like most?

What do you dislike most?

Draw a picture of your feelings.

What does your drawing tell you about how you see yourself emotionally?

What do you do to feel:

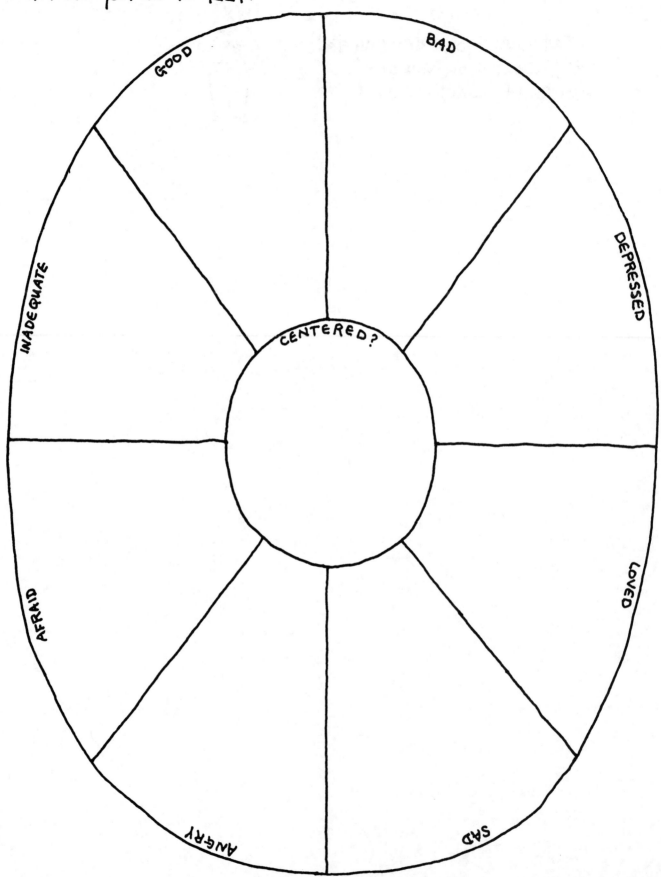

Answer these quickly without "thinking."

- I'm happiest when

- Someday I'm going to

- When I'm really down, what I want to do is

- I feel anxious when

- I'm afraid that

- I like people who

- All it takes to make me happy is

- What I really want to do is

- I wish that

- I don't like people who

- A person really should

- I just hate it that

- I have everything I need, however

- If I could do whatever I wanted, I would

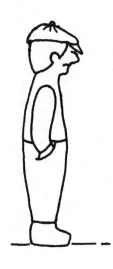

What makes you the saddest?

What might you do to take care of the part of you who feels the sadness?

When do you get punished?

How do you get punished?

When are you good to yourself?

How are you good to yourself?

What are you like when you're alone?

62.

 What do you do to be good to someone or to take care of someone?

Will you do those things for you?

When do you feel defensive?

How do you defend yourself? What is your favorite defense?

What are you most insecure about?

How has this insecurity affected your life?

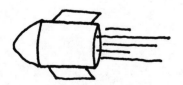

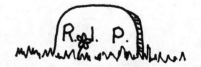

What makes you feel secure?

☞ Refer back to page 22

Reduce your list of ten
to the three things you consider most important.

1.

2.

3.

What would you like to:

HAVE?

DO?

BE?

Can you give yourself permission to have, do and be those?

What stops you? How do you stop yourself?

How do you get disappointed?
(See if you can identify the _process_ of disappointment.)

What do you expect or assume about your life
that causes you to be dissatisfied?
(Can you remember specific examples in which your assumptions and
expectations about life caused your dissatisfaction and suffering?)

How do you change when you're in a group? What does this change do for you?

How are you with someone you like ?

And with someone you dislike ?

Have you noticed that when you're with someone you like, you like yourself? And, of course, when you're with someone you dislike, not only do you dislike them, you dislike you, too?

It is true that what we like about others are the things we like about ourselves, and what we dislike in others are the things we dislike in ourselves.

We like or dislike the way we _feel_ around others. Just for fun, the next time you're with someone you dislike, keep your attention focused on accepting, approving of, and liking yourself and see what happens.

* to love but not...

* to cry but not...

* to be angry but not...

* to play but not...

* to do what I want but not...

* to have what I want but not...

* to let go but not...

* to be loved but not...

* to feel good but not...

I'll allow myself

How have you changed in the last year?

How do you feel about the changes?

When did you first experience (recall the circumstances)

LOVE	ENVY
FEAR	ANXIETY
HATRED	COURAGE
GUILT	JEALOUSY
EMBARRASSMENT	JOY

When do you presently experience

LOVE	ENVY
FEAR	ANXIETY
HATRED	COURAGE
GUILT	JEALOUSY
EMBARRASSMENT	JOY

How old do you feel when you experience

LOVE	ENVY
FEAR	ANXIETY
HATRED	COURAGE
GUILT	JEALOUSY
EMBARRASSMENT	JOY

Who in your life comes to mind when you consider

LOVE	ENVY
FEAR	ANXIETY
HATRED	COURAGE
GUILT	JEALOUSY
EMBARRASSMENT	JOY

Draw a picture of your mind.

What does the drawing tell you about how you see yourself mentally?

Complete the following:

I'm the kind of person who...

I'm the kind of person who...

I'm the kind of person who...

I'm the kind of person who...

Describe one thing about yourself that you wish were different

Name the part of yourself who wants to be different.
What are her/his primary concerns?

We cannot experience anything other than our own experience. For example, how would you know you wanted peace in your life if you didn't already know what peace feels like? When you're experiencing peace, it's coming from within you, you're "doing" peace. And this is true of anything else you might be "looking for." Love, happiness, contentment, well-being, all come from within.

Nothing external needs to change for you to have what you want. Example: Wealth is an attitude of mind. Rich is the ability to enjoy fully. Neither has anything to do with money or possessions. Many people have a lot of money but can't enjoy it because they're too worried about getting more or losing what they have.

So, if you're looking for something, do/be that. Also, don't waste your time feeling bad for not doing it before now.

If you want to be happier ⇒ be happier.
If you want to be more relaxed ⇒ relax.
If you want more friends ⇒ be friendly.

Sounds simple.

It is.

The trouble with me is... (Fill this space if you can.)

The good things about me are... (Fill this space if you can.)

What are the three things you appreciate most about yourself?

84.

Draw a picture of yourself the way you like yourself least.
Describe the qualities of this person.

Who (which part of yourself) believes there's something wrong with you? Give her/him a name.

Describe the qualities of this part of yourself.

What is s/he afraid of?

What do you get out of maintaining this belief?

Write down three "positive" opinions.

1.

2.

3.

Write down three "negative" opinions.

1.

2.

3.

Explore each to determine the "pay-off" for maintaining it. What do you gain? What do you lose?

How do you determine what is positive and what is negative?

We assume that "positive" opinions are good for us. We're taught that we "should" have them, and yet when we look closely our positive opinions often lead to as much suffering as our "negative" ones. Many of the rules, standards, and beliefs that operate our daily lives have never been examined by us from an adult point of view. It's often helpful to examine not only what we do, but also how we know to do it.

Write down three things:

I believe
1.

2.

3.

I think
1.

2.

3.

I know
1.

2.

3.

What difference do you experience in these?

When do you feel safe?

When do you feel unsafe?

Describe and/or draw the place where you feel safest.

Identify an issue.

WRITE IT DOWN IN HERE ⬆

Jot down the beliefs you hold on to around this issue.

Jot down the beliefs you push away around this issue.

Can you name the parts of you who are on each side of this issue?

In this exercise we're asking you to explore how your belief systems and assumptions can conflict and therefore keep you stuck. For example, perhaps a part of you has been conditioned to believe: "If I keep working at it, I can pretty much arrange my life the way I want it to be." Another part, differently conditioned, might believe: "I don't have any real power. I'm just a pawn in this giant socio-political game and nothing I do makes any difference." The difficulty comes when we're not aware that different parts of us hold precisely opposite beliefs.

As we pay attention to when opposing parts of ourselves are present, we can begin to see how they work to keep us right where we are, spinning our wheels, frustrated, and often puzzled.

One should...

I should...

People should...

You should...

We should...

They should...

Who said so?

Each of us has chosen a set of principles and values by which we live. (By the way, it's good to explore these to be sure we really choose them and haven't simply been told they are true.) There are things in our lives that are so in opposition to our principles and values that we cannot imagine them as options for ourselves. However, most of what we hold on to and push away has little to do with ethics and morals and much to do with liking and disliking. Often we hold on to something that makes us miserable out of a sense of pride and identity. Expressions like "you can't teach an old dog new tricks" and "never give an inch" are examples. "I'm too old to change." "I've always done it this way." ".This is just the way I am." Poor reasons.

These beliefs and others like them support your ideas of who you are. If you look closely, you might see that you are paying too high a price just to keep this identity intact.

Give something new a try. You might have fun!

Imagine the ideal you...

How does she/he look?	What are her/his qualities?
How is she/he different from you?	**What would you have to give up to be the ideal you?**

What is the best thing that could happen to you?

What is the worst thing that could happen to you?

I would be happy if only...

I wouldn't suffer if only...

My life would be perfect if only...

I wouldn't be angry if only...

My life would have been better if only...

I would have what I want if only...

I would be a better person if only...

Inside each of us is a "persistent voice of discontent." It talks in terms of "if only's" and can never be satisfied. Its function is to keep you feeling as if there is always something missing, always something just beyond your reach, which, if only you could get to it, would finally bring you contentment.

What do you think would happen
    if you stopped
    believing this voice?

Create an "Add List."

Mention every good thing you can think of about
yourself
-all that you do, love, enjoy, give, offer -
-all good deeds and works, present and past-

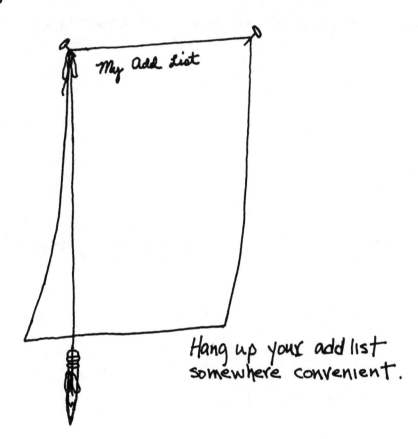

My Add List

Hang up your add list
somewhere convenient.

Add something to it every day.

 What was the nicest thing ever said about you?

What was the worst thing ever said about you?

What is the nicest thing you say about yourself?

What is the worst thing you say about yourself?

How do you give difficult information?

How do you hear difficult information most openly?

Imagine the ♡alentine you would like to receive.
– DRAW THE VALENTINE. –
Employ colors, paste, glitter, ribbon, flowers, chocolate, etc. if you'd like.

Draw a picture of your family.

What do you notice?

What do you appreciate most about the way you were raised?

What is your favorite childhood memory?

What does it tell you about who you are now?

List ☆ your ☆ father's

positive qualities	negative qualities

List ☆ your ☆ mother's

positive qualities	negative qualities

Watch to see how you exhibit each of these qualities in your life.

· · · · · · If your mother were writing an in-depth description of you,
· what would she say?

·········If your father were writing an in-depth description of you,
······························what would he say?

Remember,

these are your projections, your ideas about how someone sees you.
Look carefully at what you've written and see how this is how the part
of you who is like your mother sees you, and this is how the part of
you who is like your father sees you.

The most important thing my
FATHER
ever told me was...

The most important thing my
MOTHER
ever told me was...

How did your mother maintain distance between herself and you?

How did your father maintain distance between himself and you?

How do you maintain distance between yourself and others?

★ What needs to be done? ★ How do you know it needs to be done? ★ Which part of you needs it? ★ How long have you known this needs to be done? ★ What are you doing toward getting it done? ★ How are you stopping yourself from getting it done? ★

★ Will you do it? ★

Write a one-page definition of what a relationship is.

If you have people in your life who are willing to do this exercise, share your definitions. How are they similar? Different?

Picture yourself as you are in a relationship.

— WRITE AND/OR DRAW A DESCRIPTION. —

Picture yourself as you are not in a relationship.

- WRITE AND/OR DRAW A DESCRIPTION. -

How should a relationship be?
(LOOK CLOSELY. GIVE ALL THE DETAILS YOU CAN.)

List the major relationships in your life.

What are/were the hard places?

Which part of you does/did the relationship?

What needs are/were met?

In each one:

What do/did you learn?

What needs aren't/weren't met?

What patterns are you aware of?

How would the other person describe you?

What do you want in a relationship?

What won't you give?

What have you stopped risking?

My biggest problem in a relationship is...

What is your pay-off for having this problem?

What would you need to do to let go of it?

What stops you?

What do you say,
how do you act,
in order to get close to others?

What do you say,
how do you act,
in order to keep   others   away?

As you consider people in your life, past and present, are you sensing the patterns? It might seem quite accidental or coincidental that we seem always to wind up with the same kind of person, but it's not. Most of us have a very finely tuned sense of which people "fit" and which don't. It's important to keep in mind that we are each, in all of our life situations, first and foremost, maintaining our identity.

However, that identity seems often not in accord with what we say we want. For instance, I complain about a lack of intimacy in my relationships but continue to pick people who are unavailable, uncommunicative, workaholics, etc. If I continue to make that same choice, it would be good to consider that perhaps it is I who am avoiding intimacy. I complain about being overweight but continue to choose eating over exercising. I complain about not having enough time to myself but continue to take on responsibilities.

As we explore the patterns and the pay-offs for having them, we get closer to the underlying identity we're protecting.

What are the "wedges" you most often use to avoid intimacy?

How do you use these wedges?

When do you use them?

How could you feel safe enough to let go of them?

Write a dialogue between:

- the part of you who wants to be CLOSE
- the part of you who wants to keep a d·i·s·t·a·n·c·e.

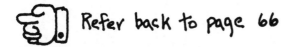 Refer back to page 66

Decide which is the most important
thing in your life.

☞ How does this make you feel?

Review your life and make a list of commitments you have kept.
(We couldn't decide whether to leave a large space or a small space
for this answer.)

Which part of you

• makes commitments? _____

• keeps commitments? _____

• breaks commitments? _____

What have you wanted to commit to and continually found yourself unable to commit to?

MARRIAGE · CHILDREN · RELIGION

CHARITY · POLITICS · EDUCATION

What would you need to do in order to make that commitment?

Relationship...

What could you commit to at this time?

What would you expect in return?

What would you have to give up in order to have a relationship?

Create a new model for a relationship.

How would others respond to it? ✳

What would you have to give up to have it?

What would you have to allow yourself to have it?

Why don't you do it?

✳ Remember that what you project onto others is true for you and not necessarily true for them.

What are you looking for?

I am looking for...

How would you like your life to be?

In order to have that...

What would you have to let go of?

What would you have to accept?

What are you willing to do?

Write a dialogue between: The part of you who is willing to change.

The part of you who is not willing to change.

You are going away for a long time alone...

What do you want to have with you?

Are there any surprises about what you forgot to list or the order in which you thought of things?

What could you "not live without"?

—WRITE AND/OR DRAW YOUR ANSWER.—

134.

Consider the many different types of "goodbyes" in our lives.

Finish these sentences:

Saying goodbye is

Saying goodbye is

Saying goodbye is

Saying goodbye is

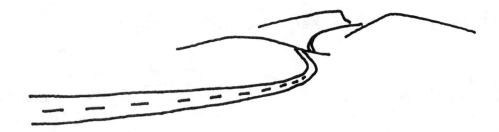

What does goodbye mean to you?

How do you say goodbye?

What do you feel with goodbyes?

How have goodbyes been in the past?

How could you take care of yourself through a goodbye?

What kinds of things help you with goodbyes?

writing a letter?

reviving old memories?

giving a gift?

packing away old memories?

Something else?
How do these things help you?

Think of a person, situation, experience from your past that you can't seem to let go of. Write a "letter of closure" expressing everything you need to express in order to put this issue to rest.

Is there something you did in the past that is deemed unacceptable? Revisit that incident, see it through the eyes of compassion, and rewrite the narrative of the experience from this perspective.

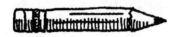

Even if someone or something

no longer present is involved,

we can find resolution within ourselves

through acceptance.

Recall a time when you let go.

- WRITE AND/OR DRAW THAT EXPERIENCE. -

Describe your spiritual life.
-WRITE AND/OR DRAW YOUR ANSWER -

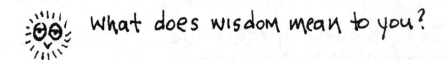 What does wisdom mean to you?

List some wise things you have heard. How does this wisdom affect your life?

How are you wise? It's very wise to recognize wisdom.

Draw a picture of your center.

What does your drawing tell you about how you experience yourself spiritually?

Which part of you drew your center?

Recall a time when you felt centered.

Centering...

What do you focus on?

What do you let go of?

Where is your attention?

What are you not paying attention to?

What happens with your
  body?

  feelings?

  mind?

From our center comes wisdom and compassion. Our center is wisdom and compassion. This is our higher Self, our True Nature, a more universal or cosmic identity. From center comes a sense of well-being, calm, peace, joy, comfort, and confidence. Life is no longer a question of I, me, mine versus you, yours--life is us and ours.

Coming from our center, we can see what is. Resistance falls away. Being here, now, present, accepting what is. No illusion of separateness. All.

Life is not a struggle, not a contest. Center is what's there when you stop doing everything else.

Life is. You are.

Those are not incompatible states.

Recall a time when you did something
you thought you couldn't do.

148.

Look back over a difficult period and let yourself re-do it the way it would have been if you had known then what you know now.

Let yourself recall something you consider unfinished.

Would you like for it to be finished?

How could you finish it?

- WRITE AND/OR DRAW -

How much of life do you allow yourself to enjoy?

How do you keep yourself from enjoying your life?

Write a prescription for yourself that will heal a dis-ease or discomfort you are currently suffering.

DR. FEELGOOD
1270 PEACEFUL ST.
SERENITY, CA

Let an image come to you that represents the relationship between your body, feelings, mind, and center.

Draw the image.

What does this drawing convey to you?

Draw a picture of death.

If you knew you had only one month to live, how would you spend it? Would you live differently from now? Are there things you'd feel an urgency to do?

Are you afraid of dying? Of death?

Which parts would you talk about with a friend?

What would you not talk about?

Are there things you'd want to clear up with others before dying?

Your life is a movie.

-Imagine the ending. Who will play you? What will your final line be?-

157.

★ Think of one thing you'd like to do before you die. ★

✪ ANSWER THESE QUESTIONS ✪
How would you feel doing it? How would you feel having done it? What will you have if you do it? What stops you?

⬇

You have lived your life and you are now very old.
Looking back over your life, what do you regret?

Is there something you could do <u>now</u> to avoid that regret?
If so, write down the steps you're willing to take.

160.

Where are you now in your life?

Where would you like to be at the end of your life?

Where will you be at the end of your life if you continue as you are now?

What do you need to let go of in order to be where you want to be at the end of your life?

162.

How did you do this workbook?

Were there exercises you skipped?

Does looking at the exercises you skipped tell you anything about yourself?

What kinds of feelings came up as you contemplated the questions?

As you read each exercise, did you judge them in any way?

Are there some you're attracted to doing again?

Would you answer them differently?

Are there some you'd answer the same?

Did your answers ever surprise you?

Did "different people" answer different questions?

How can you tell?

Can you appreciate yourself for having made this effort?

- NOTES -

- NOTES -

- NOTES -

- NOTES -

- NOTES -

Work with Cheri Huber

Visit www.cherihuber.com to access Cheri's latest interviews.

Read Cheri's blogs at http://cherispracticeblog.blogspot.com.

To talk with Cheri, call in to Open Air, her internet-based radio show. Archives of the show and instructions on how to participate are available at www.openairwithcherihuber.org

To work with Cheri on an individual basis, sign up for her email classes at schedule.livingcompassion.org.

Visit www.recordingandlistening.org to learn about the practice that is Cheri's passion.

Cheri's books are available from your local independent bookstore or online at www.keepitsimple.org.

Living Compassion

For more information on Zen Awareness Practice and the teachings of Cheri Huber, visit www.livingcompassion.org. Here you can:

- Find a schedule of retreats and workshops
- Locate meditation groups in your area
- Find out more about virtual practice opportunities such as Reflective Listening, Virtual Meditation, Email Classes
- Access newsletters and blogs on Zen Awareness Practice
- Sign up for individual or group Recording and Listening Training

Contact

Living Compassion/Zen Monastery Peace Center
P.O. Box 1756
Murphys, CA 95247
Email: information@livingcompassion.org

There Is Nothing Wrong with You
An Extraordinary Eight-Day Retreat
based on the book
There Is Nothing Wrong with You:
Going Beyond Self-Hate
by Cheri Huber

Inside each of us is a "persistent voice of discontent." It is constantly critical of life, the world, and almost everything we say and do. As children, in order to survive, we learned to listen to this voice and believe what it says.

This retreat is eight days of looking directly at how we are rejected and punished by the voices of self-hate and discovering how to let that go. Through a variety of exercises and periods of group processing, participants gain a clearer perspective on how they live their lives and on how to find compassion for themselves and others.

This work is challenging, joyous, fulfilling, scary, courageous, demanding, freeing, loving, kind, and compassionate—compassionate toward yourself and everyone you will ever know.

For information on attending, contact:
Living Compassion/Zen Monastery Peace Center
P.O. Box 1756
Murphys, CA 95247
Email: information@livingcompassion.org
Website: www.livingcompassion.org

What You Practice Is What You Have is a follow-up to
There Is Nothing Wrong with You. Here, Cheri further
exposes the lies and antics of self-hate. Included are
Awareness Practice tools, such as Recording and
Listening, for seeing how we are trapped in old patterns
of suffering and for transcending self-hate through
kindness. ISBN 9780971030978

WHAT UNIVERSE ARE YOU CREATING?

ZEN AND THE ART OF
RECORDING AND LISTENING:
A 52-CARD DECK & GUIDEBOOK

CHERI HUBER & ASHWINI NARAYANAN
AUTHORS OF I DON'T WANT TO, I DON'T FEEL LIKE IT

Acceptance

What Universe Are You Creating? is a playful, powerful way to learn the skill of Recording and Listening, a revolutionary tool for practicing turning attention from incessant, haranguing, karmically conditioned patterns of thought and action to the peace of presence. Recording in your own voice and then listening to kind words, encouragement, inspirational readings, favorite songs, gratitude lists, meditations—in short, being your own mentor—turns attention away from the constant stream of negative self-talk, robbing it of its power by revealing its illusory nature. ISBN: 9780991596300

Fear is not what we think it is. It is possible to find within ourselves the experience of life that was ours before we were taught to be afraid. *The Fear Book* shows us how to recognize fear for what it is and how to overcome its devastating effects through a series of awareness practice exercises, including the powerful Recording and Listening tool.
ISBN: 9780991596324

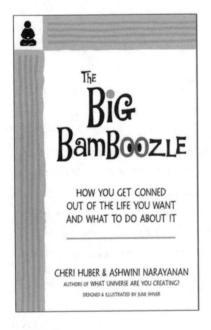

Written in a humorous and lighthearted style, *The Big Bamboozle* illustrates through essays, stories, and examples what keeps us from choosing love, happiness, and joy. The book includes a year of practical exercises and nuggets of wisdom from those who have practiced with these teachings.
ISBN: 9780991596317